A Doll's House
Classroom Questions

A SCENE BY SCENE TEACHING GUIDE

Amy Farrell

SCENE BY SCENE
ENNISKERRY, IRELAND

Scene by Scene
11 Millfield, Enniskerry
Wicklow, Ireland.
www.scenebysceneguides.com

Ordering Information:
orders@scenebyscene.ie

A Doll's House Classroom Questions/Amy Farrell. —1st ed.
ISBN 978-1-910949-01-6

Contents

Act 1 - Points to Consider

- It is interesting to consider the terms Torvald uses when speaking about his wife and the fact that he has forbidden her to eat sweets. It helps establish how he views her and gives an insight into their marriage.

- Discussion surrounding both Nora's character and her marriage are essential at this early stage to give students the basis for comparison in the play's final Act. Students often judge Nora to be silly and superficial at this early stage.

- The nature of the friendship between Nora and Kristine Linde is worth discussing. Nora claims to be firm friends with her, yet seems to know little of her life. This gives an insight into Nora's personality that students may be quick to pick up on.

- Nora reveals her secret borrowing to Mrs. Linde in this Act. This is significant for a number of reasons; she is proud to have saved her husband's life and she has broken the law to do so. Students often comment on the fact that this secret is one she cannot tell her husband, for fear it will damage their relationship.

- Differing experiences of and views of marriage are presented in the exchanges between Nora and her old friend Mrs. Linde, which are worth drawing attention to and discussing.

- Dr. Rank's comments about Krogstad as being 'morally sick' are significant, for his 'crime' was the same as Nora's.

- Considering Nora's role as a mother is rewarding after reading this Act. It helps develop students' sense of her character, and is something to revisit at the play's end.

Act 1 - Questions

1. "Is that my little squirrel frisking about?", "My little sing-
    ing bird mustn't go drooping her wings, eh?"
    How does Torvald refer to Nora? What do you think of
    this?

2. "It's incredible how expensive it is for a man to keep such
    a pet."
    Describe the relationship between Nora and Tor-
    vald Helmer in the 1st Act. Support your answer with
    quotation.

3. "Didn't go nibbling a macaroon or two?"
    Would you consider Torvald to be a controlling husband?
    Explain.

4. How have circumstances changed for the Helmers finan-
    cially since the previous Christmas?

5. What is the relationship between Nora and Mrs. Linde?

6.   "And didn't he leave you anything?"
Comment on Nora's question.

7.   What kind of relationship did Mrs. Linde have with her husband?

8.   "Dear, kind Daddy! I never saw him again, Kristine."
Comment on this.

9.   Why did Nora and Torvald visit Italy and how did they finance the trip?

10.   Why did Mrs. Linde marry her husband?

11.   Why has Mrs. Linde come to see Nora?

12.   How has Nora managed to pay off her debts to date?

13.   Why is Nora so determined to keep her borrowing a secret?

14.   "But it was tremendous fun all the same, sitting there and working and earning money like that. It was almost like being a man."
Comment on Nora's statement.

15.   Why is Nora so optimistic and upbeat in the 1st Act?

16.   How does Dr. Rank describe Krogstad?

17.   Describe Nora's relationship with her children.

18.   Explain the relationship between Nora and Krogstad.

19.   At one point Nora says, "Please, Torvald, I never get anywhere without your help". Comment on this statement.

20.   Torvald remarks, "Practically all juvenile delinquents come from homes where the mother is dishonest." Comment on this statement.

21.   Describe the Helmers' home and household.

22.   What is bothering Nora as the Act closes?

Act 2 - Points to Consider

- Nora is very concerned and agitated as the Act begins. She asks the maid whether she thinks the children would forget her if she were to leave. This gives an insight into how Nora is thinking and coping with the stress of the potential discovery of her crime.

- Dr. Rank's illness introduces the idea of children suffering because of their parents' misdeeds and is worth noting.

- Students' views of Torvald's character will be developed in this Act. His views towards women and treatment of Krogstad are both interesting discussion topics.

- Nora's dismissal of Dr. Rank's profession of love may seem both cold and childish. It can be interesting to discuss what it says about her personality and the true nature of her relationship with Dr. Rank.

- Krogstad threatens Nora and has the potential to ruin her marriage. However, he is not exactly a typical villain, something worth discussing and assessing.

- Discussing Torvald's treatment of Nora is worthwhile at this point, before the revelations of the final Act. It is worth considering whether he is justified in treating her as he does.

Act 2 - Questions

1. How does Nora show her agitation as the Act begins?

2. Do you think Nora cares a lot about her children? Explain.

3. "Torvald says I should".
   Comment on this.

4. "He's got something seriously wrong with him, you know. Tuberculosis of the spine, poor fellow. His father was a horrible man, who used to have mistresses and things like that. That's why the son was always ailing, right from being a child."
   Comment on Nora's view of Dr. Rank's illness.

5. "You see Torvald is so terribly in love with me that he says he wants me all to himself. When we were first married, it even used to make him sort of jealous if I only as much

as mentioned any of my old friends from back home."
When you hear this, what do you think of Torvald?

6.	"A man's better at coping with these things than a woman…"
How do you react when Nora says this?

7.	"If it ever got around that the new manager had been talked over by his wife…"
What does this tell you about Torvald's attitude to women?

8.	"He thinks he has every right to treat me as an equal, with his 'Torvald this' and 'Torvald that' every time he opens his mouth. I find it extremely irritating."
What do you think of Torvald's treatment of his old friend?

9.	"Why should I suffer for another man's sins?"
What does Dr. Rank mean by this?

10.	Comment on the relationship between Nora and Dr. Rank.

11.	Nora complains to Dr. Rank about his confession of his love for her by saying, "that you had to go and tell me… When everything was so nice".
Comment on this line and what it says about Nora's sincerity.

12.	Nora tells Dr. Rank, "you can see how it's a bit with Torvald as it was with Daddy."
What does this tell you about male-female relationships in the play?

13.   How does Krogstad threaten Nora?

14.   What means of escape has Nora been contemplating?

15.   What does Krogstad hope to get out of this?

16.   "Tell me what to do, keep me right – as you always do".
Comment on Nora's relationship with her husband.

17.   "The child must have her way".
What is your opinion of how Torvald treats his wife?

Act 3 - Points to Consider

- Students tend to enjoy the back-story of Krogstad and Mrs. Linde and the extra dimension it adds to the story. Their past also helps further discussion of marriage as a theme in the play, as Mrs. Linde left Krogstad, who she loved, and married for security.

- Mrs. Linde's conversation with Krogstad helps to show him as human, not just as a threat to Nora.

- Students tend to anticipate that Mrs. Linde is going to intercede on Nora's behalf and ask Krogstad to retrieve his letter to Torvald. Many will feel astonished when Mrs. Linde doesn't take this course of action and will accuse her of being a 'bad friend'. They may feel that it is easy for Mrs. Linde to judge what is best for Nora, but that a true friend would protect her.

- Torvald's descriptions of Nora at the party and after Mrs. Linde leaves, lend themselves well to the idea that she is a 'trophy wife' and that theirs is a superficial relationship, based on fantasy.

Nora's belief that a 'miracle' will happen furthers this fantasy element – her view of her husband does not match the man himself, just as his view of her is not in fact, reality.

- Torvald's view of women is displayed in comments he makes throughout this Act and these are worth noting and discussing. Lively discussion may result from some of his offhand and derogatory comments.

- Students often find the Helmers' reaction to the news of Dr. Rank's imminent death, to be quite shocking. Neither of them appear to be moved by the news, pointing to the superficiality of their relationships and the poor quality of friendship they offer.

- Torvald's self-centred reaction to reading Krogstad's letter often angers students. They may be outraged by the way he judges and condemns Nora, overlooking her motive and explanations. His intention to hush everything up and proceed with their marriage as a mere façade, also tends to agitate students and makes for lively classroom discussion.

- When Torvald opens Krogstad's second letter, his reaction that 'he's saved' and has forgiven Nora, tends to further annoy students. His behaviour here is interesting to discuss in the context of the theme of marriage in the play.

- Nora's response to Torvald here shows the hidden depths of her character and her own self-discovery. Students often begin to view her more positively, as she realises the true nature of her life and marriage.

• Nora's decision to leave Torvald can be divisive; some students will be delighted that she is leaving her sexist, conceited husband, while others will judge her harshly for her decision to leave her children with a man she claims to barely know. It can be interesting to hear students' views on this point, as many will find the ending problematic.

• Themes of marriage, love, duty and equality are worth discussing as the play ends.

Act 3 - Questions

1. What do we learn about Krogstad and Mrs. Linde as the Act opens?

2. What proposal does Mrs. Linde have for Krogstad and how does he react to it?

3. What doubts does Krogstad have about Mrs. Linde?

4. "No, Nils, don't ask for it back."
   Why doesn't Mrs. Linde protect her friend?
   What is your reaction to this development?

5. Why does Torvald think Mrs. Linde should take up embroidery?

6. Torvald calls Nora, "my most treasured possession."
   Comment on this.

Scene by Scene

Scene by Scene guides are written by teachers, for teachers. The aim of this guide is to be a time-saving resource, helping busy teachers to prepare classes and set homework. We hope this guide leads to enjoyable lessons and rewarding classroom experiences, for teachers and students alike.

About the author

This guide's author, Amy Farrell, is a secondary school English teacher from Co. Wicklow, teaching in north County Dublin since 2004.

Scene by Scene Series

Hamlet Scene by Scene

King Lear Scene by Scene

Macbeth Scene by Scene

Romeo and Juliet Scene by Scene

Shakespeare Scene by Scene Volume 1

Classroom Questions Series

A Doll's House Classroom Questions

Animal Farm Classroom Questions

Foster Classroom Questions

Good Night, Mr. Tom Classroom Questions

Martyn Pig Classroom Questions

Of Mice and Men Classroom Questions

Pride and Prejudice Classroom Questions

Private Peaceful Classroom Questions

The Fault in Our Stars Classroom Questions

The Old Man and the Sea Classroom Questions

The Outsiders Classroom Questions

To Kill a Mockingbird Classroom Questions

The Spinning Heart Classroom Questions

Visit www.scenebysceneguides.com to find out more about Scene by Scene teaching guides and workbooks.